W9-ARC-204

The Countries

Spain

Kate A. Furlong
ABDO Publishing Company

J 946
Conley

visit us at
www.abdopub.com

Published by ABDO Publishing Company, 4940 Viking Drive, Suite 622, Edina, Minnesota 55435.
Copyright © 2000 Abdo Consulting Group, Inc., Pentagon Tower, P.O. Box 36036, Minneapolis,
Minnesota 55435 USA. International copyrights reserved in all countries. No part of this book may be
reproduced in any form without written permission from the publisher.

Printed in the United States.

Photos: Corbis, AP/Wideworld, Kate A. Furlong
Editors: Bob Italia, Tamara L. Britton
Art Direction and Maps: Pat Laurel

Library of Congress Cataloging-in-Publication Data

Furlong, Kate A., 1977-
    Spain / Kate A. Furlong.
       p. cm. -- (The countries)
    Includes index.
    ISBN 1-57765-388-2
       1. Spain--Juvenile literature. [1. Spain.] I. Title. II. Series.

DP17 .F87 2000
946--dc21

                                                                    00-038109

Contents

España 4

Fast Facts 6

Timeline 7

Spain's Stormy Past 8

The Iberian Peninsula 14

Spain's Plants & Animals 18

Spaniards 20

Products to Pesetas 24

Madrid & Barcelona 26

On the Go 28

The Spanish Kingdom 30

Spain's Celebrations 32

Cultural Life 34

Glossary 38

Web Sites 39

Index 40

España

People from Spain call their country España. It is a land with high mountains and miles of coasts. Spain's land is home to a variety of plants and animals. The land also provides Spain with valuable minerals and crops.

Spain's closeness to both Africa and Europe has given it a culture unlike any other. It is rich in music, lively dances, colorful festivals, and unusual sports. And its artists and writers are world famous.

Spanish cities are full of activity. Their businesses make a wide variety of products. People get from place to place using modern forms of transportation. And the cities' parks, gardens, museums, and theaters give Spaniards many ways to relax.

Spaniards live in a country with a long and sometimes violent history. Their country has been conquered several times by groups from all over the world. For awhile, Spain was one of the most powerful countries in Europe. Then several wars weakened Spain, and its government fell into disorder.

Today, Spain's government is strong. It is working to improve its **economy** and better the lives of its people.

Hola (hello) from Spain!

Fast Facts

OFFICIAL NAME: Kingdom of Spain
CAPITAL: Madrid

LAND
- Highest Point: Pico de Teide on the Canary Islands 12,198 feet (3,718 m)
- Lowest Point: Sea Level
- Major Rivers: Tagus, Ebro, Duero

PEOPLE
- Population: 39,167,744 (1999 est.)
- Major Cities: Madrid, Barcelona, Valencia
- Languages: Castilian Spanish, Catalan, Galician, Basque
- Major Religion: Roman Catholicism (unofficial)

GOVERNMENT
- Form: Constitutional Monarchy
- Head of State: Monarch
- Head of Government: Prime minister
- Legislature: Las Cortes Generals (made up of the Congress of Deputies and the Senate)
- Flag: Red with yellow stripe and coat of arms

ECONOMY
- Agricultural Products: Grain, vegetables, olives, wine grapes, sugar beets, citrus, beef, pork, poultry, dairy products, fish
- Mining Products: Coal, iron, pyrites, copper, lead, zinc, tungsten, uranium, mercury, potash, sylvanite, chloride
- Manufactured Products: Automobiles, ships, chemicals, toys, shoes, electrical appliances
- Money: Peseta (100 centimos equals one peseta)

Spain's Flag

A Spanish bill worth 1,000 pesetas

Timeline

35,000 B.C.	Iberians begin settling in Spain
500 B.C.	Carthaginians conquer Spain
133 B.C.	The Roman Empire conquers Spain
A.D. 415	Visigoths conquer Spain
711	Moors conquer Spain
1000	The Reconquest begins in northern Spain
1469	Queen Isabella marries King Ferdinand and unites Spain
1492	Christopher Columbus discovers the Americas, Spain soon establishes colonies there
1701	War of Spanish Succession begins
1808	War of Independence begins
1868	The military revolts against Queen Isabella II
1898	Spain loses its last American colonies in the Spanish-American War
1923	Primo de Rivera leads a coup against the government
1931	Spain becomes a republic
1936	General Franco leads a revolt against the government that starts a civil war
1939	Civil War ends and Franco becomes Spain's new leader
1975	Franco dies, Juan Carlos de Borbón named king of Spain
1977	Spain holds its first free elections in 41 years
1986	Spain joins the European Union

Spain's Stormy Past

Iberians created cave paintings, such as this bison in the Altamira cave.

People have lived in Spain for thousands of years. Spain's first people were called Iberians. They were hunters and gatherers. Over time, their societies grew more advanced. They learned to farm, raise animals, and make pottery and metal tools.

Around 1000 B.C., new groups arrived in Spain. Phoenicians came to Spain from the Middle East. And Greeks came to Spain from southern Europe. These groups set up trading posts in Spain. Celts from the British Isles also traveled to Spain. They settled on the northern coasts. Then Carthaginians from Africa arrived. They conquered Spain in about 500 B.C. and ruled it until the Romans came.

By 133 B.C., the Roman Empire had conquered all of Spain. The Romans called this part of their empire Hispania. The

Romans built cities, buildings, and roads. And they spread Christianity throughout Hispania.

In the 300s, several **Germanic** tribes tried to seize Hispania from the Romans. A tribe called the Visigoths finally succeeded in 415. They soon established their own kingdom there.

In 711, Moors conquered the Visigoths and took control of Spain. The Moors were **Muslims** from North Africa. They ruled Spain for more than seven hundred years. The Moors gave Spain excellent writers, scientists, and farmers. And they built many beautiful castles and **mosques**.

The Moors built Córdoba's Great Mosque. It has many red-and-white striped arches that are shaped like horseshoes.

The Moors and the Spaniards did not get along. The Spaniards thought Spain should be a Christian country, not a **Muslim** country. So in about 1000, Spanish Christians started to take back their lands. This is called the Reconquest.

The Reconquest began in northern Spain and spread south. It was a hard task that took hundreds of years to complete. Castile and Aragón were the most powerful Christian kingdoms. By the late 1300s, they controlled most of Spain.

In 1469, Isabella I of Castile married Ferdinand II of Aragón. Isabella became queen of Castile in 1474. Ferdinand became king of Aragón five years later. Their marriage united Spain's most powerful kingdoms.

Isabella and Ferdinand affected Spain in many ways. They began the Inquisition. It **imprisoned**, killed, or **exiled** Spain's Muslims and Jews. In 1492, Isabella and Ferdinand funded one of Christopher Columbus's voyages. On this voyage, he discovered the Americas. Spain soon established many colonies there.

After Isabella and Ferdinand, **monarchies** continued to rule Spain for almost four hundred years. Spain became the most powerful country in Europe during the 1500s and early 1600s.

During this time, Spain's American colonies flourished. They brought Spain many riches. And Spain took control of several European countries.

A Moor pays respect to King Ferdinand and Queen Isabella.

Slowly, Spain's empire began to weaken. In 1701, Britain and Austria attacked Spain. They did not like Spain's new king. Their attack led to the War of Spanish Succession, which lasted until 1714. It caused Spain to lose its European possessions.

Later, Spain faced the War of Independence. It began in 1808 when French leader Napoleon Bonaparte tried take over Spain. Spain drove out the French troops in 1814. But the war weakened Spain. Its American colonies began to **revolt**. Soon, many of the colonies won their freedom, weakening Spain further.

In 1868, the military overthrew Spain's leader, Queen Isabella II. Spain's government became a republic in 1873. But two years later the **monarchy** was brought back.

In 1898, Spain fought a war with the U.S. It was called the Spanish-American War. It lasted less than a year. But it caused Spain to lose its last American colonies.

Many Spaniards were unhappy with Spain's weak government. In 1923, General Miguel Primo de Rivera led a **coup**. Several people wanted to take power. It was a time of great disorder.

In 1931, the government held an election. Spaniards voted on whether or not to make Spain a republic. The majority of Spaniards wanted a republic. So, on April 14, 1931, a republican government took office.

General Francisco Franco

The new government was less effective than Spaniards had hoped. So, General Francisco Franco led a military **revolt** against the government in 1936. Franco's group was called the Nationalists. Their attack started a civil war.

In 1939, the Nationalists won the Civil War. Franco became chief of state. He was a **dictator**. He did not allow Spaniards to have political freedom. Franco ruled Spain until his death in 1975. Franco named Juan Carlos de Borbón to take his place.

King Juan Carlos I brought back the **monarchy**. But he also allowed Spain to become a **democracy**. In 1977, Spain held its first free elections in 41 years. Then Spain joined the **European Union** in 1986.

Today, Spain is a strong nation once more. Its democratic government has remained stable. And the **economy** is growing. These elements have improved the lives of many Spaniards.

King Juan Carlos I

The Iberian Peninsula

Spain is in western Europe. It is part of the Iberian **Peninsula**. Western Spain borders Portugal. In the northeast, Spain borders France and Andorra. Southern Spain borders Gibraltar. Southern Spain is also close to Morocco, Africa. The Moroccan territories Cueta and Melilla are part of Spain.

The Mediterranean Sea forms Spain's southern and eastern borders. The Atlantic Ocean borders Spain to the south and west. A body of water called the Strait of Gibraltar separates southern Spain from Africa. It also connects the Mediterranean Sea and the Atlantic Ocean. Northern Spain borders the Bay of Biscay.

There are islands in the waters near Spain. The Canary Islands in the Atlantic are part of Spain. The Balearic Islands in the Mediterranean are part of Spain, too.

A large **plateau** covers most of Spain. It is called the Meseta Central. Many mountains and hills border the Meseta Central. The Central Sierras mountain range runs through it.

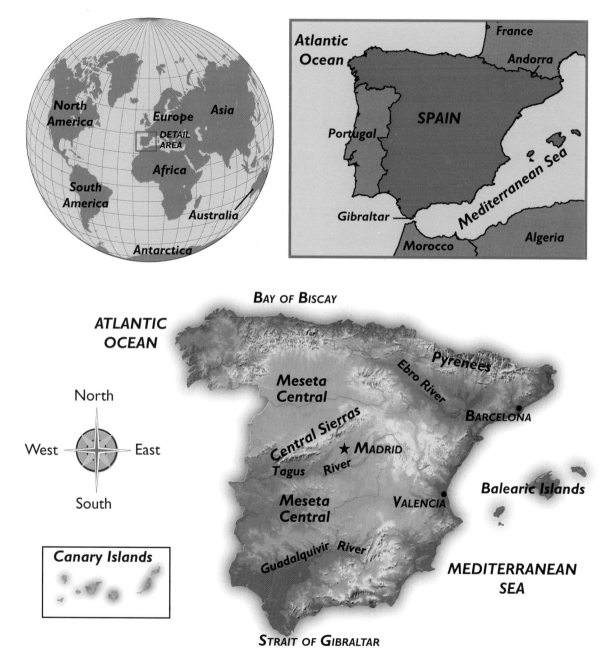

North America

Europe

Asia

DETAIL AREA

South America

Africa

Australia

Antarctica

Atlantic Ocean

France

Andorra

SPAIN

Portugal

Mediterranean Sea

Gibraltar

Morocco

Algeria

BAY OF BISCAY

ATLANTIC OCEAN

North

West

East

South

Meseta Central

Pyrenees

Ebro River

BARCELONA

Central Sierras

★ MADRID

Tagus River

Meseta Central

VALENCIA

Balearic Islands

Guadalquivir River

Canary Islands

MEDITERRANEAN SEA

STRAIT OF GIBRALTAR

The Tagus River

Spain has many rivers. The Tagus River is the longest. It is also one of the longest rivers in Europe. It is 626 miles (1,007 km) long. It flows through the Meseta Central to the Atlantic.

Mountains called the Pyrenees lie in Spain's northeast. They stretch all the way from the Bay of Biscay to the Mediterranean Sea. The Pyrenees form Spain's border with France and Andorra.

Spain has a mild climate. The coasts have hot, dry, sunny summers. Winters on the coasts are cool and cloudy. The northern coasts receive the most rain. The Meseta Central has hot, dry summers and cold, cloudy winters.

The Pyrenees

Rainfall

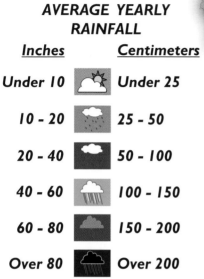

AVERAGE YEARLY RAINFALL

Inches		Centimeters
Under 10		Under 25
10 - 20		25 - 50
20 - 40		50 - 100
40 - 60		100 - 150
60 - 80		150 - 200
Over 80		Over 200

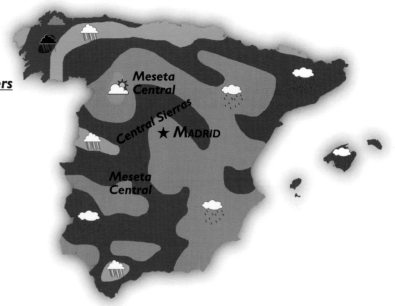

Meseta Central

Central Sierras

★ MADRID

Meseta Central

Temperature

AVERAGE TEMPERATURE

Winter

Summer

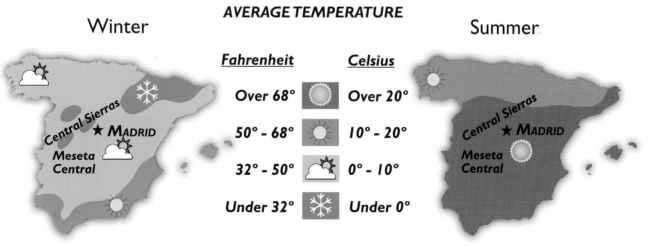

Fahrenheit		Celsius
Over 68°		Over 20°
50° - 68°		10° - 20°
32° - 50°		0° - 10°
Under 32°		Under 0°

Central Sierras

★ MADRID

Meseta Central

Spain's Plants & Animals

A pine-covered mountain slope near Catalonia

Plants cover more than half of Spain. Northern Spain has oak and beech trees. It also has **heath**. Pine trees cover many of Spain's mountains. Evergreen oaks, cork oaks, palm trees, and **scrub plants** grow well in central and southern Spain.

Spain's many national parks and nature preserves protect the country's plant and animal life. Doñana National Park protects one of Europe's rarest animals, the lynx. The lynx is a wild cat. It is shy and hunts at night. Doñana National Park also has flamingos, deer, wild cattle, and eagles.

The mountains in Spain are home to wild goats called ibexes. Ibexes live in herds. They are gray and brown. The adult males have beards and curled horns.

A young Spanish ibex

Brown bears live in the wildest parts of northeastern Spain. The largest population is at the Somiedo nature preserve. Brown bears are large and can weigh up to 550 pounds (250 kg). They can run and swim well.

A brown bear

Brown bears like to eat meat, fish, plants, and honey.

Spain's forests are home to wild boars. Boars are the largest kind of wild pig. They are covered with short, prickly hairs. They have sharp tusks and can run quickly.

Spain's waters have lots of animals, too. Dolphins, whales, and octopuses live in Spain's southeastern waters. These waters also have lots of fish such as tuna, anchovy, and swordfish.

Spain is also home to many kinds of birds. The largest birds live in the Pyrenees. These include the Spanish imperial eagle, the eagle owl, and the buzzard.

The eagle owl is Europe's largest owl.

Spaniards

Spain's long history has made it home to many people. First Iberians, Phoenicians, Greeks, Celts, and Carthaginians settled in Spain. Then Romans, Visigoths, Moors, and Gypsies lived there. Today, Spaniards are a mix of all these groups.

Spaniards are proud of their native regions. Some people feel more loyalty to their region than to the nation. Each region has its own culture. Some regions even have their own languages.

Most Spaniards speak Castilian Spanish. But three regions speak different languages. In Catalonia, people speak Catalan. In Galicia they speak Galician. And in the Basque Country, people speak Basque. All of these languages are official.

Each region in Spain has its own special foods. Some of Spain's most popular dishes are *paella* and *gazpacho*. *Paella* is a stew made from seafood, chicken, and rice. It is seasoned with a spice called saffron. *Gazpacho* is a cold vegetable soup. Spaniards also eat a lot of pork, fish, and seafood.

Lunch is Spain's largest meal. It is eaten between 2 and 3 P.M. Spaniards usually eat lunch at home. Then they take a nap called a *siesta*. Most business and stores close during this time. After the *siesta*, people return to work. This tradition is starting to fade in some of Spain's large cities.

Before dinner, some Spaniards enjoy eating *tapas*. *Tapas* are snacks. Usually they are small amounts of seasoned meat, seafood, nuts, cheeses, or olives.

A man in Pamplona cooks a pot of paella.

White houses in Andalucía

Families are important to Spaniards. Most Spanish families are made up of a mother, father, and one or two children.

Spanish families live in many kinds of homes. In Galicia, lots of houses are built of stone. In Andalucía, houses are made of baked clay. They are painted white to keep them cool. In Spain's biggest cities, people live in tall apartment buildings.

Spain has no official religion. But most Spaniards are Roman Catholics. Spain also has small groups of Protestants, **Muslims**, and Jews.

All Spanish children must attend school from ages six to fourteen. Children go to elementary school from ages six to thirteen. Then they start secondary school. It lasts for two years. Students may then choose to learn a trade. Or, they may get ready to attend a university.

After school, some Spanish students like to have a snack and relax with their friends in the plaza.

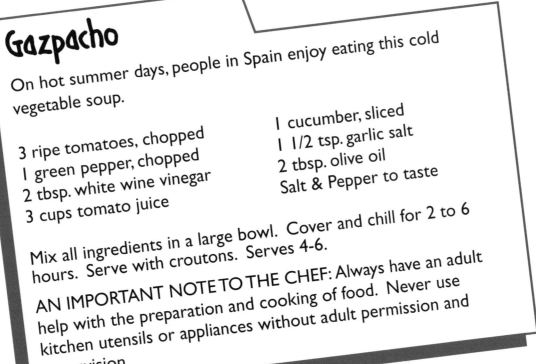

Gazpacho

On hot summer days, people in Spain enjoy eating this cold vegetable soup.

3 ripe tomatoes, chopped
1 green pepper, chopped
2 tbsp. white wine vinegar
3 cups tomato juice

1 cucumber, sliced
1 1/2 tsp. garlic salt
2 tbsp. olive oil
Salt & Pepper to taste

Mix all ingredients in a large bowl. Cover and chill for 2 to 6 hours. Serve with croutons. Serves 4-6.

AN IMPORTANT NOTE TO THE CHEF: Always have an adult help with the preparation and cooking of food. Never use kitchen utensils or appliances without adult permission and supervision.

LANGUAGE

	SPANISH	CATALAN	GALICIAN	BASQUE
Mother _____	Madre	Mare	Mai	Ama
Father _____	Padre	Pare	Pai	Aita
Hello _____	Hola	Hola	Olá	Kaixo
Good-bye __	Adiós	Adéu	Abur	Agur
Please _____	Por Favor	Si us pleu	Se fai o favor	Mesedez
Thank You __	Gracias	Gràcies	Gracias	Eskerrik asko
Yes _____	Sí	Sí	Si	Bai
No _____	No	No	Non	Ez

Products to Pesetas

Spain has a growing **economy**. It is based on agriculture, **mining**, **industry**, and **tourism**.

Before the Civil War, most Spaniards worked as farmers. Today, there are fewer farmers. But agriculture is still important to the economy.

Poor soil and little rain make farming difficult. But the farmers refuse to give up. They plant crops in nearly all of the available land.

Spain's most valuable crops are grains, such as wheat and barley. Other important crops are sugar beets, potatoes, and

citrus fruits. Spain is the world's leading producer of olive oil. It is also one of the world's largest wine producers.

Besides crops, some Spanish farmers also have livestock. They raise pigs, chickens, cows, and lambs.

A worker harvests olives from an olive tree.

Spain has one of Europe's most important **mining** industries. The largest product mined is coal. Spain is one of the world's leading producers of slate, granite, and marble. Spain also has the world's richest **mercury** mine.

Spain had little **industry** before the Civil War. But by the 1960s, Spain's industry had begun to grow quickly. Today, Spaniards build automobiles and ships. They produce iron, steel, **textiles**, and chemicals. Spaniards also make toys, shoes, and **electronics**.

During the 1960s, **tourism** grew in Spain. Visitors enjoyed the warm weather, beaches, museums, and historic cities. Tourism quickly became Spain's largest industry.

Every year thousands of tourists flock to Spain's beaches, such as this one in Cádiz.

Madrid & Barcelona

Spain's capital is Madrid. **Muslim** emir Abd ar-Rahmann II founded Madrid in the 800s. In 1607, King Phillip III made Madrid Spain's capital. It grew to become Spain's largest city.

Madrid is an important **industrial** city. Its factories make cars, planes, **electronics**, plastics, and rubber.

Madrid is Spain's cultural center. It has many museums and universities. Spain's National Library is in Madrid. And it has over 40 parks and gardens. Spain's largest bullring, Las Ventas, is located in Madrid. There are also two major soccer teams.

Madrid, Spain

People from Madrid are called Madrileños. Many Madrileños like to relax in Madrid's cafés. In the evening, they enjoy walking through Madrid's beautiful streets.

Barcelona is Spain's second-largest city. It is the capital of the **autonomous** community of Catalonia. Metals, machinery, and **textiles** are some of Barcelona's most important **industries**.

Barcelona has many cultural events. In 1992, it hosted the Olympic Games. It also has many street festivals. The festivals honor different saints. People celebrate with fireworks, music, and dance.

Young Madrileños like to take walks in Madrid's streets.

Barcelona is famous for some of its buildings that were designed by Antoni Gaudí. His buildings have unusual shapes. His greatest work is the Church of the Sagrada Familia. It has been under construction for more than one hundred years and it's still not finished!

Church of the Sagrada Familia

On the Go

Until the 1840s, it was hard to get around in Spain. The mountains blocked land travel. Shallow rivers limited water travel. People worked hard to solve these problems. Today, Spaniards travel by railways, cars, ships, and airplanes.

A high-speed AVE train sits in Madrid's Atocha Train Station.

In 1848, Spain built its first railroad. It connected Barcelona and Mataró. Soon more railroads were built. Today, Spain has two high-speed train lines called TALGO and AVE. These trains allow people to travel quickly between Spain's cities. And in Madrid, a system of subway trains called the Metro moves people around the city.

Spain built its first highway in 1967. This highway begins in Madrid. It stretches across Spain. Many cars travel on Spain's roads. Traffic can be very heavy in large cities.

Spain also depends on ships to carry its people and goods. It has the world's largest **merchant marines**. Spain's busiest ports are Bilbao, Algeciras, and Tarragona.

Air travel is another way for Spaniards to get from place to place. Forty-two airports serve Spain. Madrid's Barajas

Everyday huge cargo ships carry goods in and out of Spain's many ports.

Airport is the busiest in Spain. Spain's largest airline is called Iberia. Iberia flies within Spain. It also flies to other countries.

Iberia has 222 aircrafts in service.

The Spanish Kingdom

When General Franco died in 1975, Spain became a **democracy** under King Juan Carlos I. The new government wrote the **Constitution** of 1978. It made Spain a constitutional **monarchy**. This means Spain's leader must follow the constitution. It prevents the leader from becoming a **dictator**.

King Juan Carlos I opens a session of Las Cortes Generales.

King Juan Carlos I serves as Spain's head of state. He represents Spain in international matters. And he is in charge of Spain's military. The king chooses the **prime minister** and **cabinet**. He can also **declare** war, sign treaties, and approve laws.

The prime minister is the head of the Spanish government. The prime minister and his or her cabinet are responsible to Las Cortes Generales.

Las Cortes Generales makes Spain's laws. It is made up of two houses, the Congress of Deputies and the Senate. Spaniards elect the members of Las Cortes Generales.

A board of judges and lawyers rule Spain's courts. There are many different kinds of courts. The highest one is called the Supreme Court.

Spain is divided into 17 **autonomous** communities. Each has its own government with a lawmaking body, president, and Council of Government.

The Basque Country is an autonomous community. Its people want to form their own country. The Spanish government is against this idea. So, a group called the Basque Homeland and Liberty (ETA) uses **terrorism** to fight the government.

Spain's Autonomous Communities

All Spaniards are represented by a red flag with a wide yellow stripe across the middle. On the mast side of the yellow stripe is Spain's coat of arms. It represents Spain's historic kingdoms.

Spain's money is called the peseta. The peseta can be broken into 100 centimos.

Spain's Celebrations

Spain celebrates its official national holiday on December 6. It is called **Constitution** Day. This day honors the Constitution of 1978, which made Spain a **democracy**.

Spaniards celebrate New Year's Day on January 1. On New Year's Eve, lots of Madrileños gather at a town square called Puerta del Sol. When the clock strikes twelve, they eat one grape for every ring of the clock's bell. They believe this will bring them good luck in the new year.

Girls buy grapes for New Year's Eve (above).
Penitents walk in a **Semana Santa** *procession (below).*

In the spring, Spaniards celebrate *Semana Santa* (Holy Week). It takes place the week of Easter. Spaniards line the streets to watch a religious procession. The people in the procession carry large statues of Jesus and the saints. **Penitents** in robes and tall pointed hoods walk alongside the procession.

October 12 is Hispanic Day. This day honors Christopher Columbus's discovery of the Americas. People in the U.S. celebrate Columbus's discovery, too. But it is called Columbus Day, and it is celebrated on the second Monday in October.

Spaniards also celebrate Christmas Eve and Christmas Day. But, the most important day of the Christmas season is January 6. It is called the Day of the Three Kings. Children receive Christmas presents on this day. Their presents are from the Three Kings instead of Santa Claus.

Each year, towns hold their own special festivals. Usually the festival honors the town's **patron saint**. The festivals have music, dancing, and bullfights.

In July, Pamplona holds one of Spain's most well-known festivals. It is called the Fiesta de San Fermín. Every day there are bullfights. Before the bullfights, the bulls run through the streets. People run in front of the bulls, trying to dodge the bulls' horns.

Pamplona's festival draws thrill-seekers from all over the world.

Cultural Life

Spain is home to many famous artists. Over the years, El Greco, Diego Velázquez, Francisco de Goya, and Pablo Picasso have contributed to Spanish art. Today, Picasso is considered one of the world's finest modern artists.

The work of Spanish artists can be found in the country's many museums. Spain's leading museum is the Museo del Prado. It has more than 3,000 paintings. The museum called Centro del Arte Reina Sofía has a valuable collection of modern Spanish art. It has Picasso's famous painting about the Spanish Civil War, *Guernica*.

Guernica **shows the pain and suffering of Spain's Civil War.**

Spain has also produced important written works. In the early 1600s, Miguel de Cervantes Saavedra wrote *Don Quixote*. It is the world's first modern novel. It is about the adventures of Don Quixote and his friend Sancho Panza. More recently, five Spaniards have won the **Nobel Prize for Literature**.

Miguel de Cervantes Saavedra

Many Spaniards like to relax by watching television or going to the movies. The most well-liked television programs are game shows, soap operas, dramas, sports, and movies.

Spaniards also enjoy listening to many kinds of music, including pop and rock. Music from the U.S. and other parts of Europe is also popular.

In traditional Spanish music, people play guitars and **castanets**. Each region has its own style. Spaniards have created lots of dances to go with their music. Some popular Spanish dances are the bolero, fandango, and jota.

Another popular dance is called flamenco. It is a fast Gypsy dance that began in Andalucía. Male dancers click their toes and heels. Female dancers use their hands and bodies to express themselves. The dancers perform to guitar music.

Sports are also popular with Spaniards. One of Spain's traditional sports is bullfighting. Fans gather in an arena to watch a person called a matador fight a bull. The matador wears black slippers, tights, and a decorated suit called a *traje de luces* (suit of lights). The matador swings a cape to catch the bull's attention. When the bull draws near, the matador tries to kill it with a sword.

Female flamenco dancers wear brightly-colored dresses.

A matador uses his cape to attract the bull.

Some Spaniards think bullfighting is cruel and unfair to the bull. But many Spaniards still enjoy bullfighting and think of it as an art form. They enjoy watching the matador's skill and courage.

Spaniards also enjoy other sports. Watching and playing soccer has become popular with many Spaniards. They also enjoy basketball, tennis, hockey, and motorcycle racing.

In the Basque Country, people invented a ball game called jai alai. Players catch and throw a hard rubber ball with a long, curved scoop called a *cesta*. The players try to catch the ball in their *cesta* and return it before it hits the floor more than once.

Spain's arts and sports reflect the country's long history and its great blending of people. They have given Spain its rich, exciting culture.

A jai alai player uses his cesta to catch the ball.

Glossary

autonomous - an area, region, or community that has the right to govern itself.

cabinet - a group of people who act as advisors to a head of state.

castanets - wooden instruments that are held in the hand and clicked to make music.

citrus - fruits rich in vitamin C. They include oranges, grapefruits, lemons, and limes.

constitution - the laws that govern a city, state, or country.

coup - a sudden act that brings about a change in government.

declare - to make a formal public announcement.

democracy - a kind of government where people hold the power. They are represented by elected officials.

dictator - a ruler who has complete control and usually governs in a cruel or unfair way.

economy - the way a country uses its money, goods, and natural resources.

electronics - devices that use electricity, such as radios, televisions, and computers.

European Union - an organization of European countries that works toward political, economic, governmental, and social unity.

exile - forcing someone to leave their country.

Germanic - the people of northwestern Europe, such as the Germans and Scandinavians.

heath - open land with low-growing shrubs and plants.

imprison - to put someone in prison.

industry - the production of a large number of goods by businesses and factories.

merchant marines - ships used in business.

mercury - a silver-white, liquid, metallic element. It is used in thermometers.

mining - removing minerals from the earth.

monarchy - a government controlled by a king or queen.

mosque - a Muslim house of worship.

Muslim - a person who follows Islam. It is a religion based on the teachings of Mohammed as they appear in the Koran.

Nobel Prize for Literature - an award for someone who has made outstanding accomplishments in literature.

patron saint - a saint believed to be the special protector of a church, city, state, or country.

peninsula - land that sticks out into water and is connected to a larger land mass.
penitent - a person who is sorry for sinning or doing something wrong.
plateau - an area of flat land.
prime minister - the highest-ranked member of a government.
revolt - a movement against a state, country, or ruler.
scrub plants - low, small trees and shrubs.
terrorism - the use of terror, violence, or threats to frighten people into submission.
textiles - of or having to do with the designing, manufacturing, or producing of woven fabric.
tourism - the act of touring or traveling for pleasure.

Web Sites

Virtual Journey of Spain
http://www.ontheline.org.uk/explore/journey/spain/spindex.htm
This site provides visitors with information on Spain's culture. It has sections about sports, arts, crafts, music, dance, food, and daily life.

Spain: A Country Study
http://lcweb2.loc.gov/frd/cs/estoc.html
The Library of Congress sponsors this site on Spain. It has exhaustive information on Spain's history, society, economy, government and politics, and military.

CIA: The World Factbook 1999 — Spain
http://www.odci.gov/cia/publications/factbook/sp.html
This site by the CIA offers up-to-date statistics on Spain. It has sections on Spain's geography, people, government, economy, communications, transportation, military, and transnational issues.

These sites are subject to change. Go to your favorite search engine and type in "Spain" for more sites.

Index

A
Abd ar-Rahmann II 26
agriculture 24
Andorra 14, 16
animals 4, 18, 19
art 34
Atlantic Ocean 14, 16
Austria 12
autonomous communities 27, 31

B
Balearic Islands 14
Barcelona 27, 28
Basque Homeland and Liberty (ETA) 31
Bay of Biscay 14, 16
Bonaparte, Napoleon 12
Britain 12
bullfighting 26, 33, 36, 37

C
Canary Islands 14
Carthaginians 8, 20
Celts 8, 20
Central Sierras 14
Cervantes Saavedra, Miguel de 35
children 22
Christmas 33
Church of the Sagrada Familia 27
Civil War 13, 24, 25, 34
climate 16
colonies 10, 11, 12
Columbus, Christopher 10, 33
Constitution Day 32
Cortes Generales, Las 30

D
dance 4, 36
Day of the Three Kings 33
Don Quixote 35

E
economy 4, 13, 24
El Greco 34
European Union 13

F
family 22
Ferdinand II, King 10
festivals 4, 27, 32, 33
Fiesta de San Fermín 33
flag 31
flamenco 36
food 20, 21
France 14, 16
Franco, General Francisco 13

G
Gaudí, Antoni 27
Gibraltar 14
government 4, 12, 13, 30, 31
Goya, Francisco de 34
Greeks 8, 20
Guernica 34
Gypsies 20

H
Hispania 8, 9
Hispanic Day 33
houses 22

I
Iberian Peninsula 14
Iberians 8, 20
industry 24, 25, 26, 27
Inquisition 10
Isabella I, Queen 10
Isabella II, Queen 12

J
jai alai 37
Juan Carlos I, King 13, 30

L
language 20

M
Madrid 26, 27, 28
Mediterranean Sea 14, 16
Meseta Central 14, 16
mining 24, 25

Moors 9, 10, 20
museums 4, 25, 26, 34
music 4, 35, 36

N
Nationalists 13
New Year's Eve 32

P
peseta 31
Phillip III, King 26
Phoenicians 8, 20
Picasso, Pablo 34
plants 4, 18
Portugal 14
Primo de Rivera, General Miguel 12
Pyrenees 16, 19

R
Reconquest 10
religion 22
Romans 8, 9, 20

S
school 22
Semana Santa 32
Spanish-American War 12
sports 4, 36, 37
Strait of Gibraltar 14
Supreme Court 31

T
Tagus River 16
tourism 24, 25
transportation 4, 28, 29

V
Velázquez, Diego 34
Visigoths 9, 20

W
War of Independence 12
War of Spanish Succession 12